Tell Me in Five Words

STEPHEN RICE

Copyright © 2022 Stephen Rice
All rights reserved
First Edition

Fulton Books
Meadville, PA

Published by Fulton Books 2022

ISBN 978-1-63985-392-2 (paperback)
ISBN 978-1-63985-393-9 (digital)

Printed in the United States of America

Preface

"Tell me in five words"—the concept sounds simple enough. It may be difficult to believe, but it has taken years to write this book. I am glad you have this book. This is a book for people who don't like to read. Reading it will be time well spent. It's a true saying that even though life is good, it is ultimately neither fair nor equal. Don't let that discourage you, though. Keep going in this life. You can do something good. Believe that you can do something good to help somebody who really needs it. You can help someone today. Sometimes we all need encouragement and may find some in these pages. It is intentional that anyone can open up a random page of this book and find a five word sentence. I hope that as you read this book, you will be encouraged. You do not have to read this book in one sitting, though you probably could very easily. I believe you will find it serves you better to read a few of the sentences and then meditate on them. Then read them again. Think about your life and how the words can encourage you or how you could say those same words to encourage someone else. Call or text someone you know and encourage them with a five-word sentence. Let them know that it will get better. Let five words be the start of you sharing your testimony. Tell me in five words how good God has been to you. Tell me in five words how God set you free. Tell me in five words how God delivered. Tell me in five words how God continues to bless your life. Tell me about a loved one who kept loving you even when you were rejecting or hurting them. Tell me in five words about somebody who forgave you when you mistreated them. Tell me in five words how you forgave somebody who wronged you and how good it felt. I want you to have some five word sentences or phrases that you can use to encourage yourself. When friends walk away, encourage yourself. When loved ones die, encourage yourself. When jobs come and go, encourage yourself. When people mistreat you, encourage yourself. When people who said they would always be there walk away, encourage yourself. When you are with friends and family, encourage one another. When you are by yourself, have a five word sentence that you can use to encourage yourself so you can keep going. It will be hard sometimes, but you need to keep going. You keep going because pressing on is worth it. Keep pressing on or keep pressing in or keep pressing over or keep pressing through until you get a new blessing. Amen.

I was inspired to write this book because I have had times when I was down and needed to be lifted up; thus, I hope this book helps to lift you up. I fully admit that I can't save anybody, but I declare unto you that Jesus saves. We cannot save ourselves from our sins; Jesus Christ does that. Every day he saves me from myself. You can read in 1 Corinthians 14:19 (NLT), "But in a church meeting I would rather speak five understandable words to help others than ten thousand words in an unknown language." Paul is talking about a church meeting or worship service in this verse. It is not especially helpful to speak an unknown language to a person, but it can be particularly helpful to tell someone "Jesus can save you now." I hope you are inspired to have five words for any situation that will encourage you and not just for a church service. Some people speak in tongues as a regular gifting, but that only edifies the speaker. It does the average person no good if you don't understand what a person is saying. I want to do something that can help somebody in just a few words. So to be able to speak five words to someone that they can understand not just in worship, as Paul mentions, but in everyday life—words that they can use to be encouraged when times are hard and to live out their faith—that is what has driven this book. I hope that these words will encourage you and that you can commit them to memory to encourage yourself. Not everyone will love you, but you must love yourself. Your life may not matter to a whole LOT of people, but it must matter a WHOLE LOT to you, and it matters A WHOLE LOT to God. I hope that alone encourages you to do something good. For some people, this book will serve to plant seeds, while for others, it will water seeds already planted. Either way, I thank God that it will be Him that causes the increase. I pray that this book blesses you immensely.

Stephen Rice

1. Jesus can save you now.

2. Father, Son, and Holy Ghost

3. Greater things I will do.

4. Greater things you will do.

5. Yes, Jesus paid it all.

6. God will protect his children.

7. Jesus is coming back again.

8. If I can help somebody.

9. Lord, please help my unbelief.

10. God can use me today.

11. Lord, help me to grow.

12. I need thee every hour.

13. I'm blessed in this city.

14. I'm blessed in this field.

15. Every day you live, blessed.

16. I really love the Lord.

17. Lord, thank you for salvation.

18. Thank God for the food.

19. One day, He'll come back.

20. One day, Jesus comes back.

21. Can Jesus count on you?

22. Jesus can count on me.

23. You can count on Jesus.

24. Can Jesus count on me?

25. Holy Spirit, please teach me.

26. Holy Spirit, make me better.

27. God, make me like you.

28. This day, I choose Christ.

29. Today I serve the Lord.

30. My life belongs to God.

31. My heart belongs to God.

32. I give God my heart.

33. I gave God my heart.

34. Lord, You are my healer.

35. Lord, you are my King.

36. Not my will; your will.

37. God, move on my behalf.

38. God, move on her behalf.

39. God, move on his behalf.

40. God, move on their behalf.

41. Lord, help me be better.

42. Lord, make me like you.

43. Lord, I need your grace.

44. Lord, I need your mercy.

45. Lord, I want your peace.

46. Lord, I need your peace.

47. Help me to bless others.

48. Help me encourage other people.

49. Help me encourage somebody else.

50. Yes, somebody got saved today.

51. Yes, somebody got healed today.

52. Thank you for your peace.

53. Lord, thank you for rest.

54. I don't drink alcohol anymore.

55. I don't do drugs anymore.

56. I'm faithful to my spouse.

57. Yes, I love the Lord.

58. Jesus is real to me.

59. And Jesus said unto them.

60. The Lord told me to.

61. The Lord saved me too.

62. Thank you for blessing me.

63. Did you help somebody today?

64. Will you trust Christ now?

65. Lord, I feel your presence.

66. Jesus is waiting for you.

67. I know I am saved.

68. God is in my heart.

69. God's love is in me.

70. Jesus loves you so much.

71. God's love is the best.

72. Yes, I will serve God.

73. I will serve the Lord.

74. He has made me glad.

75. Jesus will give new life.

76. You shall be made free.

77. You shall be brand-new.

78. Old things are passed away.

79. The Lord has redeemed me.

80. Everyday I am being saved.

81. Relationships with God are real.

82. Don't be a false prophet.

83. I *was* on the corner.

84. He *was* on the corner.

85. She *was* on the corner.

86. They *were* on the corner.

87. God blessed me with work.

88. God opened up a door.

89. The Lord cleaned me up.

90. The Lord turned me around.

91. I still go to church.

92. Many people go to church.

93. Many people are saved today.

94. Many people believe in Jesus.

95. I believe in Jesus Christ.

96. God will supply all needs.

97. This is a faith test.

98. God can still do greater.

99. Do you still believe God?

100. Will you be faithful today?

101. Will you choose Jesus today?

102. Will you love your neighbor?

103. Lord, help me to love.

104. Lord, help me to stand.

105. Today I read my Bible.

106. There was a miracle today.

107. I am a living miracle.

108. Yesterday I read my Bible.

109. I love the Lord too.

110. Jesus is sho'nuff alive today.

111. Jesus can save him too.

112. Jesus can save her too.

113. Jesus can save them too.

114. Yes, your sins are forgiven.

115. You can be healed today.

116. God still heals and saves.

117. You are blessed and favored.

118. You shall do greater things.

119. You shall do greater works.

120. God is working through you.

121. God is working on you.

122. God is working in you.

123. Read the Word of God.

124. Temptation can be overcome daily.

125. God can increase your faith.

126. Grace is a good thing.

127. Mercy is a good thing.

128. Lord, give me more grace.

129. Lord, give me more love.

130. Lord, give me your Spirit.

131. Lord, I want your Spirit.

132. Jesus help me mirror you.

133. Jesus, make me like you.

134. Let me love like you.

135. Help me love others too.

136. Lord, help me to forgive.

137. Your grace is sufficient today.

138. His grace is sufficient today.

139. God's grace is sufficient today.

140. Holy Spirit, you are love.

141. Saved, sanctified, Holy Spirit-filled

TELL ME IN FIVE WORDS

142. Covered in Jesus's saving blood

143. Protected by the Lord Jesus

144. Protected by my Savior Jesus

145. I am redeemed by Jesus.

146. The abundant life is free.

147. Use me for kingdom work.

148. Help me help somebody else.

149. Deliver me, O Lord, today.

150. Strengthen me, that I stand.

151. Strengthen me, that I work.

152. Strengthen me today, O lord.

153. Lord, increase my humble faith.

154. Sing a song to God.

155. Pray for those in need.

156. You do something good today.

157. You read your Bible today.

158. Devote time to prayer today.

159. Devote time to God today.

160. Did you pray this morning?

161. Did you stop and pray.

162. God can make you new.

163. God makes the crooked straight.

164. God will make it alright.

165. In the beginning God made.

166. God took the alcohol taste.

167. God delivered me of alcohol.

168. God delivered me of sin.

169. I celebrated my salvation birthday.

170. I have accepted Jesus Christ.

171. I am satisfied with Christ.

172. I am satisfied with Jesus.

173. Do what the Lord says.

174. You should read your Bible.

175. You should read the Bible.

176. God can use anybody today.

177. God can use old people.

178. God can use young people.

179. God uses willing vessels today.

180. My brother got saved today.

181. My sister got saved today.

182. My mother got saved today.

183. My father got saved today.

184. My cousin got saved today.

185. My uncle got saved yesterday.

186. My aunt got saved yesterday.

187. I prayed for you today.

188. I prayed for you yesterday.

189. Somebody prayed for me today.

190. I will pray for you.

191. I have prayed for you.

192. I've been praying for you.

193. Rejoice, God is with you.

194. I Rejoice and am glad.

195. Lord, release your glory here.

196. Praise him for his greatness.

197. Praise him for his creation.

198. Praise him for his love.

199. Praise him for his gifts.

200. Thank God for this opportunity.

201. Thank you, Lord, for today.

202. Satan is a defeated adversary.

203. God can help you grow.

204. God loves all his children.

205. You can receive salvation today.

206. God will protect us daily.

207. God will keep us daily.

208. Angels will carry me home.

209. There is peace with him.

210. Be encouraged—He is within.

211. You matter to our God.

212. Jesus died for you too.

213. Jesus died for him too.

214. Jesus died for her too.

215. Your life matters to God.

216. My life matters to God.

217. My life matters to Jesus.

218. Heaven rejoices at my salvation.

219. All lives matter to God.

220. Jesus can deliver you now.

221. Heaven is my eternal home.

222. Heaven is your eternal home.

223. At my appointed time, heaven.

224. When I leave earth, heaven.

225. When I leave earth, gloryland.

226. When I leave earth, hallelujah.

227. One day, off to glory.

228. Grace and yet more grace.

229. Mercy and yet more mercy.

230. He will provide for you.

231. Become a child of God.

232. Use your gifts for God.

233. God has work for you.

234. Give God what is His.

235. Glad I belong to God.

236. Glad I am saved today.

237. Come on, let's praise Him.

238. God can heal the land.

239. Yes, my Bible is right.

240. Don't be ashamed to pray.

241. Don't be ashamed of God.

242. Don't be ashamed of Jesus.

243. I need God's grace today.

244. You need God's grace today.

245. God is gracing you now.

246. Right now, you need grace.

247. Jesus knows how you feel.

248. Holy Spirit, you guide me.

249. Holy Spirit, teach me well.

250. Holy Spirit, testify of Jesus.

251. Spirit of truth, lead me.

252. Spirit of God, mold me.

253. Spirit of God, fall afresh.

254. God, help me to forgive.

255. Lord, help me to forgive.

256. Redeemed by the lamb's blood.

257. I have a godly relationship.

258. A relationship with the Lord.

259. I take care of you.

260. Serve the Lord with conviction.

261. Serve God with your heart.

262. God works within you daily.

263. God works on us daily.

264. Jesus can pick you up.

265. I will be with Jesus.

266. You can be saved too.

267. God parted the Red Sea.

268. The Spirit gives perfect gifts.

269. The Spirit teaches all things.

270. The Spirit testifies of Jesus.

271. God's peace is real peace.

272. You shall be made free.

273. Have you had a Pentecost?

274. Will you love him today?

275. Yes, He loves you today.

276. He loves today and forever.

277. God can still heal you.

278. God can still do miracles.

279. God still reigns over me.

280. My soul belongs to God.

281. My life belongs to God.

282. Jesus died for me too.

283. Jesus died for you too.

284. Holy Spirit, teach me today.

285. Holy Spirit, guide me today.

286. I will do God's will.

287. Jesus fed thousands of people.

288. Jesus, betrayed by a friend.

289. Jesus resurrected the third day.

290. God gave his Holy Spirit.

291. In the beginning was God.

292. The Spirit saves you daily.

293. I saw somebody get saved.

294. Baptized by the Holy Spirit

295. Baptized by Holy Spirit fire

296. Filled with the Holy Ghost

297. Baptized in the Holy Ghost

298. Baptized by Holy Ghost fire

299. Holy Ghost and fire baptism

300. Somebody will get saved today.

301. The disciples were with Jesus.

302. The apostles were with Jesus.

303. Faith helps me each day.

304. Lead me, O great God.

305. God, you are my healer.

306. Jesus will make a way.

307. You must have real faith.

308. Have faith and believe.

309. Lord, make me like you.

310. Lord, make me perfectly yours.

311. Lord, make me your servant.

312. I want to be holy.

313. I am wholly yours, Lord.

314. You will have hard tests.

315. You shall be an example.

316. I let my light shine.

317. Let your light shine today.

318. You let your light shine.

319. Shine your light before others.

320. Be light to the world.

321. Shine the light of Jesus.

322. The world needs your salt.

323. Shine your light right here.

324. Jesus is waiting for you.

325. God is waiting for you.

326. I can't live without God.

327. With God, you have life.

328. With God, you can live.

329. Jesus gives the abundant life.

330. Life with God is better.

331. Life with Jesus is better.

332. Life is better with Jesus.

333. Life is better with God.

334. God is greater than obstacles.

335. I'm saved from my sins.

336. You're saved from your sins.

337. It will get better soon.

338. It will be better, friend.

339. God will make it better.

340. The Lord will fix it.

341. The Lord heals your body.

342. The Lord saves your soul.

343. Jesus is still the Lord.

344. Jesus has shed his blood.

345. The blood of Jesus works.

346. The blood of Jesus cleanses.

347. The blood of Jesus saves.

348. The blood of Jesus heals.

349. The blood can still deliver.

350. My savior loves us all.

351. My savior justifies me too.

352. His grace is plenteous, brother.

353. His grace is plenteous, sister.

354. His grace is plenteous, friend.

355. His grace is plenteous, sir.

356. His grace is plenteous, ma'am.

357. Jesus wants to bless you.

TELL ME IN FIVE WORDS

358. Jesus wants to heal you.

359. Confess; he will forgive you.

360. Repent; he will forgive you.

361. Repent and believe on Him.

362. Don't die in your sin.

363. Jesus gives brand-new life.

364. He is here with you.

365. He is there with you.

366. God is greater than Satan.

367. Jesus is greater than Satan.

368. The Holy Spirit is God.

369. The Holy Spirit is Jesus.

370. I doubted, but God moved.

371. I doubted, but Jesus moved.

372. God has healed my body.

373. Jesus has healed my body.

374. Jesus has healed my sickness.

375. The Lord has healed again.

376. The Lord can heal you.

377. To be kept by Jesus

378. To be kept by God

379. Hands together and let's pray.

380. The Lord sees your tears.

381. Jesus has seen your tears.

382. God is blessing you today.

383. You are a blessed person.

384. You are God's creation.

385. God gives food to eat.

386. God will meet your need.

387. Whatever it is, God heals.

388. God is changing you, brother.

389. God is making you holy.

390. Grace, grace, and greater grace

391. You can do something too.

392. Give him all your brokenness.

393. Give him all your pain.

394. Give him all your shame.

395. Has God ever failed you?

396. Has God ever fallen short?

397. God will never fall short.

398. God will make your provision.

399. Jesus will stand for you.

400. You can be saved right now.

401. You have some spiritual gifts.

402. God has given you talent.

403. God has given you gifts.

404. God has given you wherewithal.

405. You can be holy too.

406. When times are easy, pray.

407. When times are hard, pray.

408. Thank God in all things.

409. God delivered my child too.

410. My child came home today.

411. My wife and I reconciled.

412. My husband and I reconciled.

413. God has healed my husband.

414. God has healed my wife.

415. God sent us his son.

416. The Lord called for her.

417. Jesus got up for us.

418. Your sins are in remission.

419. You can do it with God.

420. Jesus is with His people.

421. God hears the saint's prayers.

422. God hears the sinner too.

423. Jesus can help you today.

424. God really believes in you.

425. God wants good for you.

426. God wants you to work.

427. Jesus can forgive your sin.

428. Jesus forgives your sin; repent.

429. God will make it alright.

430. Jesus will protect you today.

431. Trust in Jesus the Christ.

432. God still does great things.

433. Yes Jesus healed somebody today.

434. Thousands saved in one day

435. Thousands of people saved today

436. Jesus causes people to heal.

437. Jesus causes people to forgive.

438. Somehow God made a way.

439. Jesus did it for me.

440. Jesus did it for you.

441. Jesus can do it again.

442. Jesus did it for them.

443. Jesus made me a believer.

444. God himself strong and mighty

445. His Spirit helped me stop.

446. His Spirit helped me start.

447. The Spirit speaks to mine.

448. Jesus is still speaking today.

449. Jesus is still speaking now.

450. Become a child of God.

451. Be a friend of God.

452. Daniel prayed to God daily.

453. Somebody got delivered from alcohol.

454. Somebody got delivered from drugs.

455. You can do greater things.

456. Work in your spiritual gifting.

457. Grow in your spiritual gifts.

458. You are growing in God.

459. Heaven will be my home.

460. Heaven will be your home.

461. With Jesus is my home.

462. With God is my home.

463. With Jesus is your home.

464. This world is not home.

465. One of these days, heaven.

466. I have joy with Jesus.

467. I have joy in Jesus.

468. God lives in me now.

469. Jesus lives in me now.

470. Holy Spirit lives in me.

471. Eat the Word of God.

472. Live the Word of God.

473. God lives in you now.

474. The Trinity comes to me.

475. Repent of your sins now.

476. Repent of your sins today.

477. God loves more than anyone.

478. Jesus died for you too.

479. Try fasting and praying too.

480. You can fast and pray.

481. You ought to live right.

482. Faith requires you to act.

483. Faith can be big steps.

484. Faith can be small steps.

485. Faith must also include works.

486. Believe what God has said.

487. Cultivate a relationship with God.

488. Preach so they will hear.

489. Read your Holy Bible today.

490. You can sing praise songs.

491. Your lifestyle is a sermon.

492. People want to see Christ.

493. You can show people Jesus.

494. Show the love of Christ.

495. Show the mercy of Christ.

496. Show the forgiveness of Christ.

497. Show the love of God.

498. Teach them how to love.

499. Show people God is love.

500. Show them God is love.

501. Teach them what love is.

502. Show them God is real.

503. Remember that God is real.

504. Remember that still He saves.

505. Remember that still He forgives.

506. Remember that still He heals.

507. Remember that God made you.

508. Remember God is in you.

509. You are a blessed person.

510. Your family has been blessed.

511. Your family is still blessed.

512. You are blessed even today.

513. In spite of everything, blessed.

514. The Holy Spirit is God.

515. Jesus is God in flesh.

516. Jesus died for our sins.

517. God has never failed us.

518. Jesus is coming back again.

519. Jesus is coming back soon.

520. Fast every now and then.

521. Try learning the Ten Commandments.

522. Start reading the Ten Commandments.

523. Help me love like you.

524. One day, resting in Jesus.

525. I will see His glory.

526. I will see God's glory.

527. I will see God's goodness.

528. I will see God's grace.

529. I will show God's grace.

530. I will show God's mercy.

531. I will see God's mercy.

532. Truly, I love the Lord.

533. I will show God's love.

534. I will demonstrate God's love.

535. The Lord has redeemed me.

536. The Lord is on my side.

537. He provided for the widows.

538. He has sent us himself.

539. He gives us His Spirit.

540. His Spirit gives all gifts.

541. His Spirit can change you.

542. His Spirit can heal you.

543. His Spirit will make you.

544. His Spirit will heal you.

545. God can still heal you.

546. You will have faith tests.

547. Take courage, God is still.

548. The great I Am lives.

549. The I Am still lives.

550. Humble yourself like Jesus did.

551. In the midst, still praise.

552. Jesus, joy of my life.

553. He abides with me now.

554. He abides with you now.

555. God will strengthen you.

556. When weak, he strengthens you.

557. The Spirit will encourage you.

558. The Spirit will equip you.

559. God will speak through you.

560. God can speak through anybody.

561. God is speaking to you.

562. God is speaking to us.

563. Jesus is speaking right now.

564. You can live holy today.

565. You can walk in righteousness.

566. You can walk in holiness.

567. You can live in favor.

568. You can walk in grace.

569. You can be faithful, believer.

570. Draw me near my Lord.

571. Jesus, take the pain away.

572. You can live for the Lord.

573. You can do great things.

574. You can share the Word.

575. Jesus came to save you.

576. Use your spiritual gifts today.

577. Use your gifts and talents.

578. Grow in your spiritual gifting.

579. Believe it will get better.

580. Jesus raised people from death.

581. Paul raised people from death.

582. Peter raised people from death.

583. Ezekiel saw bones come together.

584. Elisha raised people from death.

585. Day one, 3,000 people saved.

586. 5,000 people fed one day.

587. People do bad; God doesn't.

588. God used Peter in ministry.

589. Followers of Jesus do works.

590. Disciples of Christ do works.

591. What did Jesus really do?

592. Jesus washed the apostles' feet.

593. The tomb is empty today.

594. The borrowed tomb is empty.

595. Live the kingdom of God.

596. Kingdom living is abundant life.

597. Abundant life is in Christ.

598. Abundant life is in Jesus.

599. Tell God thank you today.

600. Hope is in Jesus Christ.

601. Live by God's Holy Word.

602. Get saved so you live.

603. Live for the Lord today.

604. Live for the Lord always.

605. Live for the Lord every day.

606. In Christ I do live.

607. In Christ you shall live.

608. Only in Christ you live.

609. You can bear your cross.

TELL ME IN FIVE WORDS

610. Live and rejoice this day.

611. Live; he cares for you.

612. Live the abundant Christian life.

613. Live, Jesus told him, live.

614. And you shall live good.

615. And you shall live again.

616. I shall but live again.

617. Live your life like Christ.

618. Live a Christ-centered life.

619. Live a Christ-focused life.

620. Live so you live again.

621. Jesus is the living bread.

622. Christ is the living bread.

623. Jesus is the bread of life.

624. Life is in God's word.

625. Run to the Savior today.

626. Run to the amazing God.

627. Run this Christian race well.

628. Running for the Lord above

629. Running this marathon Christian race

630. Running as God graces me

631. Running with Jesus beside me

632. Running for God without fear

633. Running to help a man

634. Running to help a woman

635. Running to help a child

636. Resting in my savior's arms

637. Resting in my savior's peace

638. Believe the Lord will come.

639. He will provide for me.

640. He will provide for you.

641. He will keep your mind.

642. Don't be afraid to preach.

643. Don't be scared of folk.

644. Don't be like the world.

645. Don't be like this world.

646. You can be like Jesus.

647. You will be like Jesus.

648. Kingdom living life for me.

649. One of these days, glory.

650. One of these days, heaven.

651. One of these days, forever.

652. One of these days, saints.

653. One of these days, peace.

654. One of these days, home.

655. One of these days, reunion.

656. One of these days, crown.

657. I shall see God's glory.

658. I am determined to live.

659. You can live like Jesus.

660. You are somebody to God.

661. Lift your voice and praise.

662. Send up your praises today.

663. Bless somebody today with kindness.

664. Bless your neighbor with kindness.

665. Bless your enemy with kindness.

666. Do good for your enemies.

667. Be good to your haters.

668. Trust God until the end.

669. God is always blessing you.

670. God loves all of us.

671. Jesus died for us all.

672. Holy Spirit, teach me all.

673. Make me more and more.

674. Make me like you daily.

675. The Word gives new life.

676. Trust in Jesus today, friend.

677. Trust Jesus will fix it.

678. Trust in Jesus the Christ.

679. Trust in Christ the Lord.

680. Trust Him in any situation.

681. Trust Him in all situations.

682. Trust Him in all things.

683. Trust Jesus in everything daily.

684. Trust Jesus will heal you.

685. Trust God to move daily.

686. In Christ put your trust.

687. Trust the Bible is right.

688. Trust that Jesus loves you.

689. Trust that God loves you.

690. Trust Jesus for your greater.

691. Trust Jesus to meet needs.

692. Trust you can be saved.

693. Trust you will see God.

694. Trust you will make it.

695. Until he returns, be faithful.

696. Until He returns, love others.

697. Until He returns, pray daily.

698. Until He returns, live right.

699. Until he returns, forgive others.

700. Until He returns, live holy.

701. Until He returns, stay humble.

702. Until He returns, do works.

703. Until He returns, have faith.

704. Until He returns, show mercy.

705. Until He returns, be gracious.

706. Until He returns, be merciful.

707. Until He returns, love enemies.

708. Until He returns, love friends.

709. Until He returns, love family.

710. Until He returns, love strangers.

711. Until He returns, love everybody.

712. Until He returns, preach it.

713. Until He returns, live it.

714. Until He returns, help somebody.

715. Until He returns, show kindness.

716. Until He returns, keep loving.

717. Until he returns, keep believing.

TELL ME IN FIVE WORDS

718. Until He returns, do love.

719. Until He returns, make peace.

720. Until He returns, He saves.

721. Celebrate the resurrection of Christ.

722. Celebrate the resurrection of Jesus.

723. God can live in you.

724. Jesus can live within you.

725. Go on and thank God.

726. You have a special purpose.

727. God delivered then and now.

728. God can still deliver you.

729. God can still deliver them.

730. God still loves us all.

731. Believe Jesus still loves you.

732. Believe in Jesus Christ today.

733. Believe in Jesus Christ forever.

734. The Holy Ghost still comforts.

735. Jesus, make me like you.

736. Holy Spirit, make me holy.

737. Holy Ghost, live in me.

738. God can make you love.

739. God can help you forgive.

740. The Holy Spirit gives gifts.

741. The great gift of grace

742. The great gift of love

743. The great gift of forgiveness

744. The great gift of joy

745. The great gift of peace

746. The great gift of patience

747. The great gift of anointing

748. The great gift of preaching

749. The great gift of singing

750. The great gift of praying

751. The great gift to live

752. Greatly gifted, godly people here.

753. Greatly gifted, godly people there.

754. Wisdom is a godly gift.

755. Yes, God really loves you.

756. Yes, God really loves me.

757. Yes, God loves them too.

758. Jesus died for all humans.

759. Jesus died so we live.

760. Jesus wants you with Him.

761. Jesus wants me with Him.

762. Jesus wants us with Him.

763. I want Jesus every hour.

764. I want Jesus all day.

765. I want the Lord always.

766. I am part of God.

767. Jesus, make me like you.

768. Jesus help me make it.

769. Jesus, I love you too.

770. Thank Jesus for the anointing.

771. Thank God for anointing you.

772. Thank God for anointing me.

773. We assemble ourselves for worship.

774. We share the good news.

775. Share the Jesus good news.

776. Man, you can preach too.

777. Woman, you can preach too.

778. Live this Christian life daily.

779. Live for the Lord passionately.

780. Plant good seeds in people.

781. Plant the Word of God.

782. Water good seeds in others.

783. Let God heal your spirit.

784. Let God heal that pain.

785. Go higher in godly things.

786. Go deeper in godly things.

Rejoice

787. Rejoice when somebody gets saved.

788. Rejoice when somebody gets delivered.

789. Rejoice when somebody gets healed.

790. Rejoice when people forgive others.

791. Rejoice when people forgive others.

792. Rejoice when somebody comes home.

793. Rejoice when somebody stops drugs.

794. Rejoice when somebody ceases fornicating.

795. Rejoice when somebody ceases idolatry.

796. Rejoice for the seeds planted.

797. Rejoice for the seeds watered.

798. Rejoice for the Godly increase.

799. My name: never blotted out.

800. He humbled himself for you.

801. He will meet you there.

802. He can live within you.

803. Tell somebody about his works.

804. Teach your children God's Word.

805. Teach your grandchildren God's Word.

806. Teach your children to pray.

807. Teach your grandchildren to pray.

808. Tell strangers your favorite scripture.

809. Tell your family favorite scriptures.

810. Tell your boss about God.

811. Tell your coworkers about Jesus.

Testify

812. Testify of His loving kindness.

813. Testify of His great goodness.

814. Testify of His delivering power.

815. Proclaim Him in daily life.

816. Pray for somebody else's salvation.

817. Pray for somebody you mistreated.

818. They mistreated you, so pray.

819. They rejected you so, pray.

820. They ignored you, so pray.

821. They laughed to scorn, pray.

822. They hurt you so pray.

823. I know it hurts; pray.

TELL ME IN FIVE WORDS

Declare

824. Declare glory over your life.

825. Declare healing over your life.

826. Declare victory over your life.

827. Declare scriptures over your life.

828. Declare healing over your family.

829. Declare burdens are lifted today.

830. Declare good over your house.

831. Declare the Word daily, friends.

832. Declare God's Word daily.

833. Declare peace and healing today.

834. Declare that you are healed.

835. Declare the Word over yourself.

836. Declare the Word over others.

837. Make prayerful declarations of peace.

838. Make prayer your daily practice.

839. It's bad but gets better.

840. Jesus was a boy too.

841. Become like Jesus every hour.

842. Believe that God still can.

843. Do right by somebody today.

844. Do right by somebody tomorrow.

845. Sanctification takes place each day.

846. Salvation can happen right now.

847. Deliverance can happen right now.

848. God was with King David.

849. God was with brother Joseph.

850. God was with prophet Malachi.

851. God speaks to his own.

852. God was with the Israelites.

853. God was with the prophets.

854. Jesus was with the disciples.

855. Jesus helped a father believe.

856. Jesus helps you to believe.

857. Jesus helps with your needs.

858. The Holy Spirit gifts you.

859. The Holy Spirit equips you.

860. The Holy Spirit loves you.

861. God came through with help.

862. God came through with money.

863. God came through with grace.

864. God came through with mercy.

865. God has forgiven; forgive yourself.

866. Jesus knows how you feel.

867. Your sin hurt Jesus Christ.

868. But He still forgave you.

869. Remember, chosen for kingdom work.

870. Remember how blessed you are.

871. Remember that God fixed it.

872. Remember God healed your body.

873. Remember God sent your spouse.

874. Remember God delivered you too.

875. Remember that person he saved.

876. Remember God healed those children.

877. God's protection is yours today.

878. God gave you your job.

879. God has kept you today.

880. I will see Jesus myself.

881. You will see Jesus yourself.

882. I'll see Jesus in peace

883. I'll see Jesus in glory.

884. Don't sit on your gifts.

885. Focus on the Lord today.

886. Focus on the Lord daily.

887. Focus in your prayer life.

888. You will be tested—pass.

889. The Lord just healed somebody.

890. Somebody spoke in your favor.

891. The Lord's waiting for you.

892. You are a child of God.

893. You are anointed for this.

894. You are anointed to overcome.

895. Knowing Jesus—a beautiful thing.

896. Jesus knowing you—beautiful thing.

897. God anointed you for this.

898. God's anointing made you victorious.

899. Keep trusting and be victorious.

About the Author

Stephen Rice is a man who loves God. He also loves his family. He is not the typical ordained Christian minister. He has been writing since he was a kid. He believes in the power of books to help, teach, encourage, and inspire people. He believes in the good in people and has a zeal for ministry. He hopes that his writings will uplift you. He hopes you will be encouraged to do something good to help somebody other than yourself, and be encouraged to help somebody who really needs it. He loves to see people do better and loves to watch sports, especially football and basketball. His motto is: "No matter what happens, tell the Lord thank you and keep on going."

CPSIA information can be obtained
at www.ICGtesting.com
Printed in the USA
JSHW021301050722
27596JS00002B/69